THE CONCISE

Adair on communication and presentation skills

Edited by Neil Thomas

THOROGOOD

Published by Thorogood Publishing Ltd
10-12 Rivington Street
London EC2A 3DU

Telephone: 020 7749 4748
Email: info@thorogoodpublishing.co.uk
Web: www.thorogoodpublishing.co.uk

A CIP catalogue record for this book is
available from the British Library.

ISBN paperback: 978 185418 9233
ISBN ebook: 978 185418 9240

Special discounts for bulk quantities
of Thorogood books are available to
corporations, institutions, associations
and other organisations. For more
information contact Thorogood by
telephone on 020 7749 4748, or email
us: info@thorogoodpublishing.co.uk

For information about John Adair
and products/services, see
www.johnadair.co.uk

The author and editor

John Adair

John Adair is internationally acknowledged as having had a significant influence on management and leadership development in both the business and military spheres. He has seen military service, lectured at Sandhurst, worked extensively as a consultant, held professorships in Leadership Studies and authored critically acclaimed management and leadership books which have sold in their hundreds of thousands. He has lectured at conferences all over the world. (www.johnadair.co.uk)

Neil Thomas

Neil Thomas is Chairman of the Falconbury group of companies that comprises, Falconbury Ltd (www.falconbury.co.uk), Management Forum (www.management-forum.co.uk) and Thorogood Publishing Ltd (www.thorogoodpublishing.co.uk). He has been involved in publishing and seminars/training for most of his business life. He gratefully acknowledges the assistance of Angela Spall, Editorial Director of Thorogood in the preparation of the *Concise Adair* series of books.

Contents

Appendices

Introduction

It is self evident that written and spoken communication skills are of crucial importance in business (and personal) life. Managers and leaders in particular must be effective communicators, good at getting their message across to, and at drawing the best out of, people. Communication skills in all forms, including non-verbal communication, need to be worked at and improved to ensure you understand people and they understand you.

1 Defining communication

Communication is used to cover listening and talking and is a loose concept. It has its roots in Latin where its use embraced to impart, to participate and to share. It evolved as a word to mean the transmission of intangible rather than material things. But meaning comes into it too and communication might be usefully defined as:

> *the process by which meanings are exchanged between people through the use of a common set of symbols (i.e. usually language).*

However, the exchange can be of feelings and it must be noted that in this particular context emotions do not need words to be transmitted or received intentionally or unintentionally.

A workable definition of communication (for our purposes) would have these characteristics:

1 Individuals who have social contact with each other

Social contact can be face-to-face and removed (i.e. via the written word or through telephone, email, computer/tablet/smartphone, television, radio, film, video etc).

2 Shared means of communication

Usually this means through language but it also covers non-verbal communication:

- physical gestures
- eye contact
- tone of voice
- use of touching
- appearance
- facial expression
- posture
- proximity
- position of head

3 The clear transmission of a message

This means expressing oneself clearly in a way that aids understanding and overcoming any physical inhibitions (speaking or writing clearly or using the right medium).

4 Understanding of the message by the receiver

Communication has to be a two-way process and seeing it as one-way ignores the receiver's contribution to the process, and this is why assessing feedback to judge the effect and response outcome of communication is important.

2 Issues in communication

- You must be in social contact with the other person or people

- You must want to communicate

- It is better to risk familiarity than be condemned to remoteness

- The best way to empower others is to impart information (along with the delegated authority to make decisions and act on the information given)

- Get out of your office – meet, listen, provide information and give people the context in which they operate – to communicate and encourage

- Good communication is the core of customer care

- Remember customers (and suppliers) communicate with others about you

- To communicate with your customers you must handle complaints (as an organisation) as personally as possible – by a meeting or phone call in preference to letter or email; you must listen to what customers suggest and communicate product/service changes/developments with them in advance

- Presentation skills are important in communicating with colleagues as well as customers/clients

- Meetings, internal/external/online are key indicators of a person's communication (including listening) skills

- Communication is a business requirement: establish proper systems and ensure all use them

- Remember the equation: size + geographical distance = communication problems

- Communicate with poor performers to improve their contribution and in appraisals be truthful, helpful and tactful

- Help others to improve their communication skills and strive to improve them bit by bit. (Also, assess the communication skills of colleagues and identify areas for improvement.)

Personal communication
skills checklist

Answer yes or no:

1 Do you understand the importance of communication in your personal and business life?

_____

2 Are you a good communicator? (Check with your partner at home, with friends and with colleagues.)

_____

3 Can you write down your strengths and weaknesses as a communicator? And have you listed them?

_____

_____

_____

_____

_____

_____

_____

_____

4 Have you identified a need to improve your communication skills in any, or all, of these areas? Will you
now set about doing so (*reading further books and/
or attending training seminars as needs be*)?

- listening _____

- reading _____

- writing _____

- one-to-one interviews_____

- speaking and presentation _____

- managing meetings _____

- within your organisation _____

5 Are you motivated strongly to become an excellent
communicator?

_____

3 Listening

Listening has been called the forgotten skill in communication. It is more than just hearing, it is the giving of thoughtful attention to another person whilst they are speaking.

The 'disease of not listening' – the 'I hear what you say' response – exhibits the following symptoms:

- Selective listening is habit forming: not wanting to know things and turning a deaf ear to certain types of information does two things:

  i) you do not listen to important items

  ii) people censor what they tell you and both can be damaging in business and in your private life

- The constant interrupter is not listening (but planning his/her own next interruption)

- The 'day-dreamer' is not a listener

- The poor listener is easily distracted by external factors, e.g. noise, heat/cold

- The lazy listener makes no effort to absorb difficult information

- The poor listener over-reacts to a speaker's delivery and/or quality of visual aids rather than concentrating on what is being said.

The tell-tale signs of a good listener:

- paying close attention to others when they are talking

- taking an interest in someone you meet for the first time, trying to find an area of mutual interest

- believing everyone has something of value to teach or impart to you

- setting aside a person's personality/voice in order to concentrate on what they know

- being curious in people, ideas and things

- encouraging a speaker (with nods or eye contact)

- taking notes

- knowing one's own prejudices and working at controlling them to ensure listening continues

- being patient with poor communicators

- not being told you don't listen

- having an open mind in respect of other peoples' points of view

Listening skills centre on the five following attributes:

1 Being willing to listen

2 Clearly hearing the message

3 Interpreting the meaning (the speaker's meaning, not only your interpretation)

4 Evaluating carefully (suspending judgement at first but then assessing value and usefulness)

5 Responding appropriately – remembering communication is a two-way street.

In active listening you must be prepared to:

• ask questions

• weigh up the evidence

• watch your assumptions

• listen between the lines (at what is not said and for non-verbal elements such as facial expressions, tone, posture, physical gestures etc).

How better listening skills can yield dividends:

1   You can learn new ideas and acquire useful information. Lord Roy Thornson of Fleet had a childlike curiosity about everything... he pumped everyone dry on every imaginable subject. It is worth remembering that each person you meet is a potential teacher.

2   Not only does listening win you ideas and information, it can also help others and we all need to talk to people who will listen and understand worries that we or they have.

3   If you are a good listener, you help to create in others better listening skills, i.e. if you listen to others, they are more likely to listen to you.

4 Reading skills

Good reading is listening in action – giving time and thought and remaining alert to the possibilities suggested. A good reader will try to work past:

- poor structure and layout

- boring style

- off-putting tone

- too much or too little information

- difficult to follow content

- inordinate length

- lack of illustration/diagrams

You should examine what materials you **must** read, **should** read, or **might** read in the light of your job/role/ future ambitions and then decide accordingly how and when to handle a particular item.

Speed reading is useful but only if it is accompanied by speed understanding and reading too fast (or too slowly) can impair understanding.

Read selectively (according to the must, should or might categorisation) from each item that confronts you. In this, scanning can help decide what attention to give particular items, so you should look at overall content (headings and sub-headings), sample the style and content of a few paragraphs, scan (if still interested) selected parts and then read that which you decide you are interested in. In reading carefully, you should be aware of the need to:

- be clear about your purpose of reading any piece of writing

- have questions in mind

- keep the questions firmly in mind and seek answers to them

- read for main ideas

- test the evidence, explanations and conclusions critically

- make notes as you progress

- test the writer's experience against your own

- consider whether or not to re-read

- discuss the material with others if appropriate

- reflect on what has been read

"I took a course in speed reading, learning to read straight down the middle of the page, and was able to read War and Peace in twenty minutes. It's about Russia."

WOODY ALLEN

5 Writing skills

Communicating in writing is an essential part of your job. There are key elements in written communications:

- Structure and lay-out
- Content
- Style and tone

Writing should be thought of as another way of talking to a person and the six principles of good spoken communication apply – and they are:

1 Clarity

2 Planning and preparation

3 Simplicity

4 Vividness

5 Naturalness

6 Conciseness

In emails/letters, reports and memos the quality improves if the appropriate amount of planning is given to the points you wish to make and their order of importance. Further drafts can improve on the initial effort.

In writing a business email or letter you should always test the draft to ensure that:

1 the message is clear

2 points are made in the best order

3 it has the right style and tone

4 the most appropriate words and phrases are being used

5 the grammar/spelling is correct

6 the layout is attractive

In writing reports which work the following points should be borne in mind:

- If the report is to stand alone and not to support a briefing or presentation it will need to be more than an aide-memoire

- A report should:

  - have an introduction with background and set out objectives

  - a title which indicates its purpose

  - be structured like a book with chapters, headings and sub-headings all clearly numbered and well signposted

  - ensure the main body of evidence is succinct and arranged in an easy to follow order

  - end off with conclusions and recommendations

- indicate assumptions made
- put complicated data into an appendix
- use illustrations/diagrams to clarify points made

- Easy reading makes hard writing

- Churchill's guidelines for report writing centre on:

    - Setting out main points in a series of short, crisp paragraphs

    - Complicated factors or statistics should form an appendix

    - Considering submitting the headings only, to be expanded orally

    - Avoiding woolly phrases, opting for conversational phrases

    - Setting out points concisely aids clearer thinking

- Reports can be tested for their effectiveness as follows:

    - is the structure and layout clear and easy to follow

    - is the content complete and does it:

        a) state the purpose?
        b) say when, by whom, for whom and with what scope it was prepared?
        c) identify and address the problem clearly
        d) ensure detail does not cloud the main issue
        e) give sources for facts

f) use consistent symbols and abbreviations

g) use accurate figures

h) make clear statements

i) have conclusions which flow logically from facts and their interpretation

j) ensure other possible solutions are only abandoned with stated reasons?

- In general

  - is the report objective?

  - are criticisms of its recommendations pre-empted?

  - is it efficient and business-like?

  - does it offend anyone?

  - can it be understood by a non-technical person?

  - is it positive and constructive?

  - does it point up the decision to be made and by whom?

The style and tone of written communications is important to ensure the message is put over, and received, clearly. Some rules are:

- keep it simple

- strive for clarity above all things (even above brevity)

- be natural

- be concise

- let the tone reflect your true feelings but beware of being terse, curt, sarcastic, peevish, angry, suspicious, insulting, accusing, patronising or presumptuous

- be courteous (cordial and tactful).

How to keep it simple

Anyone who wishes to become a good writer should endeavour, before he allows himself to be tempted by the more showy qualities, to be direct, simple, brief, vigorous and lucid. This general principle may be translated into practical rules in the domain of vocabulary as follows:

- prefer the familiar word to the far-fetched

- prefer the concrete word to the abstract

- prefer the single word to the circumlocution

- prefer the short word to the long

- prefer the Saxon word to the Romance (i.e. Latin)

These rules are given roughly in order of merit.

H.W. and F.G. Fowler, The King's English (1906)

6 Arguing/discussion in communication

The ability to argue rationally and calmly is now almost the 'best art' in the management and leadership skills-set. However, it can be an immensely useful tool in using communication to 'trash out' ideas and solutions to any problems.

'Gentlemen, I take it we are all in complete agreement on the decision here'.

Alfred P. Sloan, the head of General Motors, looked around the committee room table. His senior managers nodded in assent.

'Then', continued Sloan, 'I propose we postpone further discussion of this matter until our next meeting to give ourselves time to develop disagreement and perhaps gain some understanding of what the decision is about'.

Several centuries earlier Shakespeare had expressed the same truth in a sentence: 'Rightly to be great is not to stir without great argument'. By 'great argument' Shakespeare meant a debate of high quality upon the reasons for and against the various courses of action. That is just what Sloan had sensed was lacking in his committee.

Personal ways of thinking it out with others vary considerably. Some managers favour an argumentative style. Take Lord Thomson. On one occasion, which must have been typical of many, Thomson took one of his senior executives, Gordon Brunton, with him to Scotland to clinch a deal.

'I recall that two days after he got back, I had him on the plane with me bound for Edinburgh and another deal, and the two of us arguing all the way north about how we should handle it. We were going to make an offer to Thomas Nelson and Sons, no less, to take over their considerable business in educational and other books. Gordon and I were arguing all the way to Turnhouse, and from the airport all the way by car to Selkirk, where we were to meet Nelson's chairman at his house. Our argument was on the point of whether the business was worth its valuation of assets or its valuation of earning power. When we stepped out of the car, and not until then, I told Gordon we would play it his way and base our offer on earnings.

In a remarkably short time we had bought the famous business – and in doing so on the basis Gordon had argued for, we had saved ourselves roughly £600,000.

'Now we will have a good dinner, I said as we drove towards Edinburgh. 'Do you like spaghetti?'

I can imagine what he expected, but I took him to a café of my earlier acquaintance, and we had soup, spaghetti, and tinned fruit salad, for which Gordon now reminds me he paid the bill of 11s. 4d. It wasn't until I was just getting into bed, having arranged for an early call so that we could skip the hotel breakfast and catch the first flight to London, that I let my thoughts wander to stamp duty. On a purchase like this stamp duty would be sizeable. I couldn't get it out of my mind and for once wasn't able to sleep. When we met in the morning I told Gordon about it and when we got on the plane we were able to take only some coffee because we had the balance sheets and accounts spread out in front of us as we anxiously calculated the situation. By capitalizing some of the assets, we could reduce the stamp duty payable, we finally decided, from £30,000 to £20,000, I was satisfied.

I don't know exactly what Gordon thought of that trip, or what he thinks of it now, although he makes occasional oblique references to it, and how he was done out of a slap-up dinner and then his breakfast, but I think he learned a lot from it. About me, anyway. About how I am always open to be persuaded.'

Thomson, like Winston Churchill, was an intuitive man with a strong personality, someone who thinks for himself and comes to some firm conclusions. Strength in this case means tenacity or perseverance. Such a person is not easily dislodged from an opinion, and perhaps never so from a conviction. He may not appear to be a good listener, but such leaders are persuadable. Paradoxically some 'good listeners', those who nod and smile at you and appear to be intent upon your words, are not in fact persuadable: they are acting a part.

The consequence is that if you wish to dislodge the Churchill or Thomson type of thinker you must be prepared to stand your ground and to argue.

Between the poles of hot, noisy argument and an academic discourse there are many positions for you to choose from. In some instances you may want to contend and disagree based upon a firm (if ultimately moveable) point of view; in others you may want to generate an atmosphere of discussion rather than argument, where each possibility is considered by presenting the considerations for and against without prior commitment upon your part or anyone else's. It depends partly on the situation, partly on the matter under consideration, and partly upon your temperament.

Whatever approach you adopt – or have thrust upon you – you should constantly remember the ends of argument. It is not to win or to avoid losing. The ends of argument are the truth, or at least greater clarity about the issue at stake or the true alternatives. The very word comes from the Latin *arguere*, to make clear. It should be essentially a rational process, a sifting of the consequences of a proposed course of action, or of several courses of action, so that the balance sheet of arguments for and against can be plainly read by the experienced and unprejudiced eye.

What is impermissible is that there should be no discussion, debate or argument in organisational life. For there will always be matters about which reasonable men and women may reasonably disagree. It is the ends and quality of the debate, more than the personal styles of those involved, which matters most.

"The great impediment of action is in our opinion not discussion but the want of that knowledge which gained by discussion prior to action. For we have a peculiar power of thinking before we act too, whereas other men are courageous from ignorance but hesitate upon reflection."

PERICLES

> "Where there is much to learn, there of necessity will be much arguing, much writing, many opinions; for opinion in good men is but knowledge in the making... Give me the liberty to know, to utter and to argue freely according to conscience, above all liberties."
>
> **MILTON**

Milton, of course, was convinced that truth existed objectively and that we tend to doubt the strength of the truth to prevail. 'Let her and Falsehood grapple; who ever knew Truth put to the worse in a free and open encounter?'

How to get it wrong

Rational argument, a 'free and open encounter', implies some rules, some common acceptance of criteria and a common commitment to truth. These will reduce the possibilities of errors, fallacies or deliberate cheating. If you encourage the winning-at-all-costs mentality, incidentally, you must expect more deliberate foul play. Tricks and cheating involve such motives, but you should also be on the alert for slipshod thinking as well. The following list of professional fouls, fallacies, slipshod thinking and pitfalls into which the unwary step, is far from exhaustive. But it gives you some idea what to look for.

1   Playing the person, not the ball – in other words, don't get personal, keep it impersonal

2   Argument by analogy – analogies always break down

3   Rationalising – in the sense of making excuses

4   Drawing irrelevant conclusions – avoid diversions, red herrings and non-sequitons and always challenge assumptions

5   Reduction to absurdity – if you argued, for example, that the less labour you employ the less cost you incur, therefore to be completely cost-effective you should employ no labour at all, you are offering a *reductio ad absurdum* for the rest of the board of directors to consider. Carrying an argument to its logical conclusion nearly always produces a nonsense.

6   The no decision/no action argument – as in 'there is much to be said on both sides, so no decision can be made either way'. Have you ever heard these 'arguments?

   • Leave it until we are not so busy

   • We're not quite ready for that yet

   • Let's hold it in abeyance

   • Let's give it more thought

   • Let's form a committee

   • It needs more work on it

- Let's make a survey first

- A working party should look into the whole area

7   All and some – i.e. avoid generalisations, although arguments in the cast of formal syllogisms, with accompanying statements like 'I am being logical now', are rare in boardrooms, there are plenty of fallacious arguments put forward in the name of reason. Many of them hinge on the use of *generalisations* followed by *deductions*.

Of course some generalisations are true, and we can deduct from them. 'All men are born' is true, therefore it is equally true that if he is a man he must have been born. But most such generalisations are suspect. 'All blue collar workers are idle' is as untrue as 'all managers are only out for the maximum possible profit'.

It is an aid to clear thinking if you insert the phrases 'tend to be' or 'have a tendency towards', if only to cover yourself. You can get away with saying that 'women tend to be intuitive', but not with 'all women are intuitive'. It is often a cause of unpopularity these days to be moderate and shun the media-catching exaggeration. But it pays off in the clarity of your thought. Caution over generalisations is not merely academic nicety. Too often decisions are based upon unwarranted statements or assumptions about what is generally the case.

Thinking revolves around the poles of the general and the particular, and getting the relationship between them as correct as possible.

Proof by selected instances is a variation of the all-and-some fallacy. Much dishonest argument consists of selecting instances favourable to our view while conveniently ignoring other instances which are either unfavourable or downright hostile to it.

One variation of the 'all and some' argument, which causes endless domestic and professional trouble, is generalising from selected instances *ad hominem*. Instead of saying accurately 'You have been late three times', you say 'You are *always* late'. Exaggerations intended for emphasis, signalled by such words as always and never, rob you of the truth and the psychological advantages that go with it.

Arguments using statistics are notoriously liable to 'all and some' errors. For it is often unclear whether or not generalisations can properly be drawn from the samples. If 3,986 people in Boston now prefer bran products to cornflakes for breakfast, can we infer that *all* Americans do? Perhaps there is more experience of cereal choice in Los Angeles.

Statistics can be biased in the first place. Cooking or laundering the figures is not unknown but more often than not it is the interpretation of the figures that is biased. In order to get the best out of this important source of data you need to be able to distinguish clearly between a *fact* and an *opinion* when these are cooked together and served up on your committee room table.

8 Middle-of-the-road arguments – i.e. the assumption that the truth lies always in the mean position between two extremes is obvious nonsense.

7 Speaking and presentation skills

Effective speaking

There are certain principles to be followed to increase the power of communicating or expressing thoughts in spoken words.

Adair's six principles of effective speaking

1 Be clear

2 Be prepared

3 Be simple

4 Be vivid

5 Be natural

6 Be concise

Preparation is helped by asking the Who? What? How? When? Where? Why? of the speaking occasion to focus on the audience, the place, the time, the reasons giving rise to the occasion, the information that needs to be covered and how best to put it across. The same principles apply to online presentations.

1 Clarity

"He could describe a complex situation with amazing lucidity and sum up a long exercise without the use of a single note. He looked straight into the eyes of the audience when he spoke. He had a remarkable flair for picking out the essence of a problem, and for indicating its solution with startling clarity. It was almost impossible to misunderstand his meaning, however, unpalatable it might be."

BRIGADIER ESSAME ON FIELD MARSHAL MONTGOMERY

2 Preparedness

Ask yourself 'What and Why and When and How and Where and Who.'

3 Simplicity

Make complex matters sound simple without talking down or being simplistic.

4 Vividness

Bring the subject to life and speak with obvious enthusiasm.

5 Naturalness

"I act best when my heart is warm and my head ..." actor Joseph Jefferson, whose advice applies to any speaker as well as actor.

6 Conciseness

Concentrate on what **must** be said rather than on what **should** or **might** be said bearing in mind the time constraints.

Presentation skills

There are six clusters which form the main elements of good, effective presentation skills.

1 Profile the occasion, audience and location
You should ask yourself these questions:

- The occasion
    - what kind is it?
    - what are the aims of it?
    - what time is allowed?
    - what else is happening?

- The audience
    - do they know anything about you?
    - do you know its size?
    - what do they expect?
    - why are they there?
    - what is their knowledge level?
    - do you know any personally/professionally?
    - do you expect friendliness, indifference or hostility?
    - will they be able to use what they hear?

- The location
  - do you know the room size, seating arrangement, lay-out/set-up and acoustics?
  - do you know the technical arrangements for use of microphones, audio-visuals, lighting and whether assistance is available (and have you notified in advance your requirements)?
  - do you know who will control room temperature, lighting and moving people in and out?
  - have you seen/should you see it?
  - check out and ensure the best location/setting for any online presentation

2 Plan and write the presentation

Elements to address are:

- Deciding your objective which needs to be
  - clear
  - specific
  - measurable
  - achievable in the time available
  - realistic
  - challenging
  - worthwhile
  - participative

- Making a plan with a framework which has:

  - a beginning (including introductory remarks, state-
    ment of objectives and relevance and an outline of
    the presentation(s))

  - a middle (divided into up to six sections maximum,
    ensuring main points are illustrated and supported
    by examples or evidence, use summaries and
    consider time allocation carefully – and test it)

  - an end (summarise, linking conclusions with objec-
    tives and end on a high note)

3 Use visual aids

As up to 50 per cent of information is taken in through
the eyes, careful consideration should be given to the
clear, simple and vivid use of audio-visuals.

Useful tips are:

- PowerPoint slides help make a point and keep eye
  contact with an audience (look at the people not the
  slides)

- Only present essential information in this way (keep
  content to about 25 words or equivalent if in figures)

- Have them prepared with appropriate professionalism

- Know the order

- Use pictures and colour if possible

- Do not leave a visual aid on for too long

Some difficulties with the different types of audio-visual equipment are:

- *PowerPoint slides/computers/DVDs, etc:* make sure you are fully aware of how to use the equipment before you begin

- *Flipcharts:* are easy to use and informal but difficult to use successfully with large groups, and generally do not look professional and take up time to use

4 Prepare your talk

In preparing your talk you need to decide whether you are to present with a full script, notes or from memory. This depends on the occasion and purpose of the presentation but whichever method is chosen, it is always acceptable to refer to your fuller notes if needs be during a presentation. Notes on cards or on slide/flipcharts/whiteboards can be used as memory joggers if you present without notes. If you are required to read a paper, at least be able to look up occasionally. Remember that failing to prepare is preparing to fail.

5 Rehearse with others

Rehearsal is important, but not so much that spontaneity is killed and naturalness suffers, to ensure the presentation (and any audio-visual aid) is actually going to work in practice.

You should always visit the location if at all possible and check that everything works – knowing the location is as important as rehearsing the presentation. Check background/privacy for online presentations.

6 Delivery on the day

Overall you should ensure that your presentation's:

- **beginning** – introduces yourself properly, captures the audience and gives the background, objectives and outline of your talk.

- **middle** – is kept moving along (indicating whether questions are to be asked as-you-go or at the end) with eye contact over the whole audience, at a reasonable pace, with a varying voice and obvious enjoyment on your part.

- **end** – is signalled clearly then goes off with a memorised flourish.

- **questions** – are audible to all (or repeated if not), answered with conciseness, stimulated by yourself asking some questions, dealt with courteously and with the lights on.

- **conclusion** – is a strong summary of talk and questions/discussions and closes with words of thanks.

If you find you are nervous (and this is normal) experiencing fear and its physical manifestations, remember to:

1   Breathe deeply

2   Manage your hands

3   Look at your audience

4   Move well

5   Talk slowly

6   Compose and relax yourself

7   Remember that the audience is invariably on your side

8   Project forward to the end of the presentation and picture the audience applauding at the end.

8 One-to-one interviews

Such meetings have the common characteristics that they are (usually) pre-arranged, require preparation and have a definite purpose.

Unless it happens to be a dismissal, one-to-one interviews require that:

- both parties know the purpose of the meeting (notified in advance)

- information to be exchanged should be considered in advance and answers at the meeting should be honest

- as interviewer you should keep control: stick to the point of the issue and the time allocated and give the other party adequate time to talk (prompting by questions if necessary).

The structure of the interview should be as follows:

- **the opening** – setting the scene, the purpose and a relaxed atmosphere

- **the middle** – stay with the purpose, listen, cover the agenda

- **the close** – summary, agree action, end naturally not abruptly on a positive note.

Sometimes it is useful to ask the right questions to obtain the required information/exchange. Questions to use are the open-ended, prompting, probing, or what-if questions, whilst the ones to avoid (unless being used for specific reasons) are the yes/no, closed, leading or loaded questions.

The skill of asking the right question

Questions are the tools of interviewing or – more widely – of listening. The art of interviewing largely consists of asking the right questions at the right time. There are several different kinds of question, each with its pros and cons. It is useful to have them all in the repertoire, so that you don't get stuck like a broken record on only one type of question.

Question	When to use	Pitfalls to avoid
The Yes/No Question e.g. 'Have you read this report?'	When checking facts	Can result in over-simplified answers
The Closed Question e.g. 'How long have you worked here?'	Where facts or data are sought	Questions that sound like an interrogation leave little room for discussion
The Open-ended Question e.g. 'How do you see your career progressing?'	To open up a discussion of information and ideas	Can result in rambling answers and irrelevancies
The Leading Question e.g. 'Don't you agree that you should have done that weeks ago?'	Only if trying to push the discussion in a certain direction	Answers are usually limited in value
The Loaded Question e.g. 'What do you think about the chief executive's stupid plan for expansion in Europe?'	Avoid unless it's deliberately provocative	Loaded questions usually have some hidden implication. Can have repercussions

Question	When to use	Pitfalls to avoid
The Prompt e.g. 'So what did you do then?'	Guides the other party in content and direction; clarifies the other persons understanding	Can prematurely curtail an interesting reply to an open-ended question
The Probe e.g. 'What precisely was the extent of your budget responsibility in Canada?'	Can be useful in obtaining specific information	Can make it sound like an interrogation
The Mirror e.g. 'So you felt completely fed up at this point?'	Useful in clarifying your understanding of the other persons reply	Be aware that you could introduce a slight alteration of meaning
The What-if Question e.g. 'Supposing we opened an office in the Gulf, would that interest you?	Creating imaginative situations can open up new thoughts	Can push someone into a corner. Only really gains hypothetical information

In performance appraisal interviews the aim should be to give constructive criticism in the following way:

1 In private

2 Without preamble

3 Simply and accurately

4 Only of actions that can changed

5 Without comparison with others

6 With no reference to other people's motives

7 Without apology if given in good faith.

In receiving constructive criticism you should:

1 remain quiet and listen

2 not find fault with the criticising person

3 not manipulate the appraiser by your response (e.g. despair)

4 not try to change the subject

5 not caricature the complaint

6 not ascribe an ulterior motive to the appraiser

7 give the impression you understand the point

In handling criticism you should accept it and not ignore, deny or deflect it.

9 Managing meetings in person/online

Meetings are much maligned, but are they usually approached and handled as they should be?

In general terms a meeting needs:

- planning
- informality
- participation
- purpose
- leadership

if it is to work, and that is so whether the meeting is in committee or conference format.

A meeting must have a purpose and this can be one (or all) of the following:

- to pool available information
- to make decisions
- to let off steam/tension
- to change attitudes
- to instruct/teach

Meetings must be prepared for:

1 Know in advance what information, reports, agenda, lay-out, technical data or equipment is required

2 Be clear about the purpose

3 Inform other participants of the purpose and share, in advance, relevant information/documents

4 Have a timetable and agenda (and notify others in advance)

5 Identify main topics with each having an objective

6 Make necessary housekeeping arrangements.

Chairing a meeting means that you should guide and control it having defined the purpose of it, gatekeeping the discussions as appropriate (opening it to some, closing it when necessary), summarising, interpreting and concluding it with agreed decisions, on time.

The chairman's role in leading/refereeing effective meetings is to ensure that the following elements are handled correctly:

1 **Aim** – after starting on time, to outline purpose clearly

2 **Plan** – to prepare the agenda (and allocate time)

3 **Guide** – to ensure effective discussion

4 **Crystallize** – to establish conclusions

5 **Act** – to gain acceptance and commitment and then to end on time.

Meetings are groupings of people and can develop their own personality. It can help to understand the personality of a particular grouping by reference to group:

- conformity
- values
- attitude to change
- prejudice
- power.

So that the method of running the meeting and making it effective depends on understanding and overcoming problems posed by the group personality.

The shortcomings of Chairman X

1 X's meetings never begin or end on time. X shows an arrogant disregard for the value of other people's time and also for their professional advice or opinions.

2 X is too fond of the sound of X's own voice. X can never say things succinctly. X's listening ability is minimal.

3 X seldom has a written agenda and never circulates one in advance. X's planning is all last- minute, usually on the back of a meeting.

continued over...

4 X has no control of the meeting – lets favourites ramble on and doesn't check topic-jumping.

5 X gives the impression that the political standing of X's section and division is the most important aspect, and many of X's meetings are concerned with delaying or avoiding decisions which may affect them adversely.

10 Within your organisation

Organisations have a degree of permanence, hierarchy and formal communication. Informal communication supplements the formal communication that is needed in organisations.

The **content** of communication in organisations should be (in relation to):

1   **The task:**
    - the purpose, aims and objectives
    - plans
    - progress and prospects

2   **The team:**
    - changes in structure and deployment
    - ways to improve team work
    - ethos and values

3   **The individual:**
    - pay and conditions
    - safety, health and welfare
    - education and training

The **direction** of flows of communication within an organisation must be downward, upward and sideways.

Decisions on what to communicate should bear in mind the must-know priorities and distinguish them from the should-know or could-know lower priorities. The best method for must-know items is face-to-face backed by the written word.

Two-way communication should be used and encouraged to:

- Communicate plans/changes/progress/prospects

- Give employees the opportunity to change/improve management decisions (before they are made)

- Use the experience and ideas of employees to the full

- Understand the other side's point of view.

11 Briefings

Briefing individuals and/or teams is an important means of communication – instructing and informing are the key elements.

The content of a briefing session is the result of carrying out the functions of defining the task and planning its implementation. After stating the objectives and why they are important you have to describe the plan – it is essential for you to answer the question which will be in everyone's minds, 'What is my part going to be?' So ask yourself before and after such a briefing meeting questions such as:

- Does everyone know exactly what his job is?

- Has each member of the group clearly defined targets and performance standards agreed between him and me?

The main purpose of a briefing meeting is to allocate tasks to groups and individuals, to distribute resources and to set or check standards of performance. Each person should know at the end what is expected of them and how the contribution of their sub-group or the individual fits in with the purposeful work of everyone else.

Effective speaking in briefings

You do not have to become a great orator. The only test is whether or not you can speak in such a way that you *move the group to the desired action*. Demosthenes said to a rival orator: 'You make the audience say "How well he speaks!" I make them say " Let us march against Philip!"'

An element of persuasion in the sense of explaining why in a convincing way will enter into most briefing or communicating meetings. But it will happen more naturally if you have mastered the skills of speaking or briefing. We can identify five sets of skills involved in briefing a group effectively for action.

Briefing skills

Skill	Definition	How you can do it
Preparing	Thinking ahead and planning your communication	Plan a beginning, middle and end to your talk. Include visual aids
Clarifying	Being clear and understandable	Put things simply and seek clarifying questions
Simplifying	Putting complex issues in an easily understandable way	Relate the unfamiliar to the familiar with simple analogies. Avoid complicated terminology and jargon. Give an overview at the start and a summary at the end
Vivifying	Making the subject some alive	Use vivid language or even gimmicks. Be enthusiastic and humorous
Being yourself	Coping with nerves and behaving naturally in front of your audience	Breathe deeply. Be aware of yourself and your nervous habits

Some of the supreme examples of leadership occur when a leader takes over a demoralised group and 'turns it around'. The initial briefing meeting can be especially important in this process. First impressions are as basic in working relationships as in love and friendship. The impression you make on people at that first meeting will stay with them forever. The task may have to be covered in general terms if you are new to the job – you can do little more than share your first thoughts. But you can share your vision, your spirit of resolve and your determination to change the climate and standards of the group. That may require some tough talking, and people will wait to see if it is going to be backed up by equally firm deeds.

On 13th August 1942 Montgomery arrived at the Eighth Army Headquarters, two months before the battle of Alamein. 'The atmosphere was dismal and dreary', he wrote in his diary. That evening he addressed the entire staff of Army Headquarters, between fifty and sixty officers. As he was their fourth Army Commander within a year, he faced a sceptical audience. They plainly doubted if he was the man to reverse their recent defeats and failures. If the morale of that broken army was to be recreated their hearts had to be won that evening.

Montgomery stood on the steps of his predecessor's caravan and bade the gathering sit on the sand. He spoke without notes, looking straight at his audience.

'I want first of all to introduce myself to you. You do not know me. I do not know you. But we have got to work together; therefore we must understand each other and we must have confidence in each other. I have only been here a few hours. But from what I have seen and heard since I arrived I am prepared to say, here and now, that I have confidence in you. We will then work together as a team; and together we will gain the confidence of this great army and go forward to final victory in Africa.

I believe that one of the first duties of a commander is to create what I call, 'atmosphere' and in that atmosphere, his staff, subordinate commanders and troops will live and work and fight.

I do not like the general atmosphere I find here. It is an atmosphere of doubt, of looking back to select the next place to which to withdraw, of loss of confidence in our ability to defeat Rommel, of desperate defence measures by reserves in preparing positions in Cairo and the Delta. All that must cease. Let us have a new atmosphere.

The defence of Egypt lies here in Alamein and on the Ruweisat Ridge. What is the use of digging trenches in the Delta? It is quite useless; if we lose this position we lose Egypt; all the fighting troops now in the Delta must come here at once, and will. Here we will stand and fight; there will be no further withdrawal. I have ordered that all plans and instructions dealing with further withdrawal are to be burnt at once. We will stand and fight here.

If we can't stay here alive, then let us stay here dead.

I want to impress on everyone that the bad times are over. Fresh divisions from the UK are now arriving in Egypt, together with ample reinforcements for our present divisions. We have 300 to 400 new Sherman tanks coming and these are actually being unloaded at Suez now. Our mandate from the Prime Minister is to destroy the Axis forces in North Africa; I have seen it written on half a sheet of notepaper. And it will be done. If anyone here thinks it can't be done, let him go at once; I don't want any doubters in this party. It can be done, and it will be done; beyond any possibility of doubt.

Now I understand that Rommel is expected to attack at any moment. Excellent. Let him attack.

I would sooner it didn't come for a week, just to give me time to sort things out. If we have two weeks to prepare we will be sitting pretty; Rommel can attack as soon as he likes after that, and I hope he does.

Meanwhile, we ourselves will start to plan a great offensive; it will be the beginning of a campaign which will hit Rommel and his army for six right out of Africa.

But first we must create a reserve corps, mobile and strong in armour which we will train out of the line. Rommel has always had such a force in his Afrika Corps, which is never used to hold the line but which is always in reserve available for striking blows. Therein has been his great strength. We will create such a corps ourselves, a British Panzer Corps; it will consist of two armoured divisions and one motorised division; I gave orders yesterday for it to begin to form, back in the Delta.

I have no intention of launching our great attack until we are completely ready. There will be pressure from many quarters to attack soon; I will not attack until we are ready and you can rest assured on that point.

Meanwhile, if Rommel attacks while we are preparing let him do so with pleasure; we will merely continue with our own preparations and we will attack when we are ready and not before.

I want to tell you that I always work on the chief-of-staff system. I have nominated Brigadier de Guingand as Chief-of-Staff Eighth Army. I will issue orders through him. Whatever he says will be taken as coming from me and will be acted on at once. I understand there has been a great deal of 'belly-aching' out here. By 'belly-aching' I mean inventing poor reasons for not doing what one has been told to do.

All this is to stop at once.

I will tolerate no belly-aching. If anyone objects to doing what he is told, then he can get out of it; and at once. I want that made very clear right down through the Eighth Army.

I have little more to say just at present. And some of you may think it is quite enough and may wonder if I am mad. I assure you I am quite sane.

I understand there are people who often think I am slightly mad; so often that I now regard it as rather a compliment.

All I have to say to that is that if I am slightly mad, there are a large number of people I could name who are raving lunatics.

What I have done is to get over to you the 'atmosphere' in which we will now work and fight; you must see that that atmosphere permeates right down through the Eighth Army to the most junior private soldier. All the soldiers must know what is wanted; when they see it coming to pass there will be a surge of confidence throughout the army.

I ask you to give me your confidence and to have faith that what I have said will come to pass.

There is much work to be done. The orders I have given about no further withdrawal will mean a complete change in the layout of our dispositions; also that we must begin to prepare for our great offensive.

The first thing to do is to move our HQ to a decent place where we can live in reasonable comfort and where the army staff can all be together and side by side with the HQ of the Desert Air Force. This is a frightful place here, depressing, unhealthy and a rendezvous for every fly in Africa; we shall do no good work here. Let us get over there by the sea where it is fresh and healthy. If officers are to do good work they must have decent messes, and be comfortable. So off we go on the new line.

The Chief-of-Staff will be issuing orders on many points very shortly, and I am always available to be consulted by the senior officers of the staff. The great point to remember is that we are going to finish with this chap Rommel once and for all. It will be quite easy. There is no doubt about it.

He is definitely a nuisance. Therefore we will hit him a crack and finish with him.

Montgomery stepped down and the officers rose and stood to attention. 'One could have heard a pin drop if such a thing were possible in the sand of the desert', recollected Montgomery. 'But it certainly had a profound effect, and a spirit of hope, anyway of clarity, was born that evening'. His Chief-of-Staff, de Guingand, agreed: 'It was one of his greatest efforts,' he wrote, 'The effect of the address was electric – it was terrific! And we all went to bed that night with new hope in our hearts, and a great confidence in the future of our Army. I wish someone had taken it down in shorthand, for it would have become a classic of its kind.' Fortunately, it was taken down in shorthand and filed away for many years before appearing in print for the first time in 1981.

Note in Monty's speech how he:

1   Set about changing the group atmosphere

2   Communicated about the common objective

3   Communicated the new outline plan to his officers

4   Set new group standards

5   Explained what he expected from all present

6   Responded to the individual needs of his staff.

The outstanding leaders of the Second World War – Eisenhower, Slim, Montgomery and Mountbatten – all practised this direct approach. They were not too busy. As young men they had suffered in the First World War under generals who never came near the front-line or left their comfortable headquarters in order to tell the subalterns and men *what* was going to happen and *why* it was important. So they resolved that if ever they rose to command armies in the war they would perform the briefing function.

Briefing the individual

Briefing individuals – giving instructions – is a perennial function of manpower and leadership. Like all functions it can be done well, in which case it becomes a skill; or it can be done badly, in which case it is called a disaster. In a crisis or an emergency, those instructions are usually given as commands or orders. Where that life-or-death element or obvious shortage of time is not there it is best to give instructions in the form of suggestions or questions. Where possible give reasons for the action.

Tony, I suggest you get that report about sales in France into the marketing director by next Friday, not the following Tuesday. I know he needs it for a Board meeting on Monday. Could you do that, please?

People tend to do things much more willingly if they are *asked*, rather than told. That is why an element of natural courtesy should flavour all that a leader does. Certainly, good leaders tend to ask you to do things – they do not boss people about.

Clearly, performing the briefing function with understanding and skill takes you well beyond the specific example of giving instructions to your team before tackling an objective. In this wider context it involves a sustained attempt in the group or organisation to let people know what is going on and to create or build a spirit of positive, constructive and confident teamwork.

Briefing checklist

- Regularly brief your team on the organisation's current plans and future developments
- Improve these five skills of briefing effectively:
  - Preparing
  - Clarifying
  - Simplifying
  - Vivifying
  - Being yourself
- Identify the most effective briefing talk by a senior manager that you have ever heard. In one sentence, why was it effective?
- Improve the two-way communication in your business of information and instructions, and identify those responsible for carrying them out

12 Coaching and communication

Coaching should be considered as one of the techniques to be used to communicate. Leaders and managers at all levels should be open to coaching of themselves and to see coaching as a way of developing others. During coaching, ideas can be communicated and clearer understanding, better knowledge, useful insights, 'savvy' and 'nous' can be shared. Coaching is a useful means to get your message across and to learn what others think.

Coaching (and the related but different technique, mentoring) require all the skills of communication, including listening, of course. Coaching is now recognised as being of great importance in the development of individuals and presents its own communication challenges.

Understanding coaching

Coaching has been described as:

'Guidance to enhance capability and skills in a particular current role and/or in anticipation of a future role. (May be internally provided – for example, by one's manager or a specialist – or provided by an external expert.)

Frequently tends to focus on the ability to manage people and change. May be developmental or remedial. By implication, needs to meet the organisation's needs as well as the individual's.'

(*Careers Research Forum 2001 Report.*)

Coaching can differ from mentoring which is usually about being a sounding board or sharing experience.

It should also be borne in mind that coaching is not counselling, which is more to do with providing support for personal issues and decisions.

Coaching need not only be of individuals but also of teams – to examine team interaction as well as individual needs.

Deciding what type of coaching is needed

This involves analysing the needs and then deciding on the type of coaching that is appropriate. For example it might be:

1. Coaching to tackle weaknesses in interpersonal skills or management style, particularly where an able individual is being held back both in their own development and the contribution they can make to the organisation by poor influencing skills and a failure to take people with them.

2. Coaching to supplement deficiencies in say leadership, people skills, IT understanding etc.

3. Coaching to prepare individuals for higher office.

4. Coaching for the induction of those new to an organisation – to introduce newcomers to an organisation and minimise future problems.

Expert coaching

Deciding what needs to be communicated should influence how the coaching is to be carried out:

- to impart specialist knowledge, e.g. presentation skills, IT, marketing, finance, strategic development;

- to increase individual self-awareness and to improve an individual's skills at interpersonal relationships;

- to improve an individual's performance in key aspects – particularly to focus on important business decision areas;

- to groom managers in having the confidence to operate at higher levels of leadership and management.

Coaching skills are usefully imported by using outside specialists for certain areas, as identified above, and where a manager is undertaking some coaching, i.e. actually carrying it out, then he/she should recognise where outside expertise is needed.

Self-help communication improvement plan

1. Make sure you clarify your ideas before communicating

The more thoroughly you analyse the problem or idea, the clearer it should become. The search for preliminary clarity is the first step toward any effective communication. Only as a result of a considerable amount of thinking (and sometimes hard wrestling with problems) does the content yield up its treasure of clarity, simplicity and vividness.

2. Test the real purpose of each communication

Ask yourself always what you really want to achieve with your message. It may be to initiate action, to win commitment, to enlarge understanding or to change attitudes. Once you have identified the most important aim – then your plan, language and tone should reflect that goal. The art of communication lies not least in the ability to fashion means to fit ends neatly and appropriately. It is necessary to define the objective as precisely as possible. A common mistake is to attempt too much in any one communication. The sharper the focus of the intention the greater its chances of being realized.

3. Be mindful of the physical and human setting whenever you communicate

This guideline embraces two key elements in communication: the recipients and the situation. The receivers bring their own past history, education, frames of reference, meanings and expectations to the communication. It is a sign of a good communicator if he or she spends as much time on understanding the recipients as on grasping the subject.

The communicator should develop a greater sensitivity to the total physical and human situation which forms the context of the actual or proposed communication. The situation is simply the particular combination of circumstances.

From the standpoint of a communicator, it is important to check your sense of timing against the situation. The circumstances in which you make an announcement or ask a question will affect its outcome. As the old saying puts it, there is a time and place for everything. If waiting is often included in the strategy of a good communicator then timing should be part of the tactics.

The principle that the situation influences the relationships of people (and therefore communication) reaches down to the physical environment too. Should you communicate in private, for example, or otherwise? Improving the physical conditions for a communication can contribute considerably to its outcome.

Within an organization this principle of assessing the 'setting' includes understanding thoroughly the total communication system, the sum of all the methods and how they interact with each other so that we know instinctively in a given situation what the appropriate channels are for sending messages upwards, downwards or sideways. This can avoid the twin errors of communicating to too few on the one hand and too many on the other.

4. Consult with others, wherever appropriate, in planning communication

One of the best and simplest ways of improving the methods you employ in communication is to discuss them and even try them out with others first. These discussions, trial runs or rehearsals may additionally throw up questions about the aim and the content, but they are especially valuable for exposing the drawbacks or weaknesses of the method employed.

As a principle, the sooner that others are involved in planning a communication the better. If it is left until the eleventh hour the form of the communication (including the audio-visual aids) may have so 'hardened' in the communicator's mind that he will be reluctant to make substantial changes. Or it may be literally too late. It is far better to present your tentative draft and sketches first and then have one or two more rehearsals later. Even if it is only a matter of asking a question or making a complaint, it is a good self-training practice, if time allows, to check the wording with someone else.

5. Always consider in any communication overtones, as well as the basic content, of your message

We should be aware that our non-verbal communication is going out from us all the time, like radio waves which the communicant can pick up. We should tune these transmissions to match our intentions by controlling the distractors, such as mannerisms. Also it involves allowing the natural tone of voice, facial expression and gesture to integrate freely with the message.

This awareness or sensitivity should extend to language as well. The emotional overtones of some words are well known: they have the power to conjure up the feelings they signify. A 'trigger' word or phrase can explode like a detonator in another person's mind. All words have their attendant aura tails; a sense of these shades of meaning can be easily developed by turning often to a dictionary. Such a habit also aids clarity.

There is also the possibility that whatever is strongly in your 'make-up' or personality, but not necessarily expressed in word or outward sign, will be picked up by the other person. Fear is especially contagious, as are all the negative attitudes or emotions, such as hostility or embarrassment.

6. Create an opportunity to convey something of help or value to the receiver

It is easy (but fatal in the long-term) to reduce this guide to a formalized and insincere ritual of 'praise first, then criticize'. A few sugary phrases of flattery before the 'But...' which starts the real point of the meeting: all too often appraisals take this unimaginative form. Yet communication depends on the strength of the line of relationship between two or more people. And the way to build up that relationship is by using it frequently to convey helpful or valuable ideas or information, so that the positive attitude behind all good communication becomes manifested.

This practice stems best from the habitual attitude of 'doing unto others as we would have them do unto us'. We like to receive helpful suggestions, or communications which enhance our own sense of the worth-whileness of our contributions. If we have made some kind of special effort we appreciate the finishing touch of a genuine 'thank-you' from those who have benefited. Yet we are often slow to take up our daily opportunities for giving help, bringing something valuable to, or showing a lively concern for, another person or persons.

It is true that communicants will be more willing to receive criticism or ill-tidings from a person whom they have grown to trust through the tenor of his general communication with them. But if they detect that this positive communication is developed only with ulterior motives in mind, the results will be disastrous. Eventually want of sincerity breeds want of trust. In a faithless atmosphere even offers of help, gifts and compliments will be greeted with suspicion and perhaps fear. If we entertain positive attitudes towards people it is natural for us to want to bring them good news or constructive help whenever we can, simply because we like them.

7. **Always follow up your communications**

We shall not be able to improve our communication unless we find out how effective it has been. You can actively follow up some communications by encouraging feedback from the receiver through asking questions and by a positive attitude to any opinions he may offer. But should you rely upon the immediate verbal feedback? Try asking the questions some days or weeks after the communication.

Another useful yardstick is to review behaviour or performance. If the original communication aimed at some change in the way someone does something, look over the heads of their initial reaction – positive or negative – and see what actually has changed. If nothing has happened the temptation is to blame the people concerned. But the communicator should first reassess his own communication to diagnose more precisely why it has failed. Did you really make clear enough the changes that were required? Did you check sufficiently thoroughly that everyone understood his part?

8. Communicate with tomorrow in mind as well as today

Communication must be aimed primarily to meet the needs of a given situation in the present. If it is to be accepted by the receiver it must also be related to the common part – social, cultural and personal. Most important of all, however, it should be consistent with the long-term interests of the future. We have to live with the consequences of today's communication in our tomorrows, be it for good or ill.

In practical language, communicating for tomorrow means the ability to speak for the purpose and aims of an organization, or individual – what they hope to do and be in the future. Of course the situation, the general conjunction of circumstances, will shape the lives of both corporations and individuals, but – as we look ahead – there is a degree of choice before us. Communicating about that choice, and the values which can act as compass bearings guiding us in an as yet unformed future, should complement the mass of daily communications which jump from moment to moment. Awareness of the future, a distinctively human characteristic, makes communication more difficult, but enriches it. Sometimes it takes courage to communicate for tomorrow, but if we can bring ourselves to do so the people of tomorrow will rise up and thank us.

9. Make your actions support your communications

Actions speak louder than words. If a person's attitudes or actions contradict their words, our tendency is to discount what they say. Thus, in industry, communication is no substitute for sound management practices on the one hand, and integrity on the other. Action in this context is a wide term, embracing a team leader showing new employees how to do the job at one end of the spectrum, to a chairman or managing director establishing proper systems or procedures for communication at the other end. An action is what you do, as opposed to what you say. Words should interpret what is done, and action should accompany words. The test of our words is whether or not we are willing, if the situation requires, to back them with action.

Thus, if you wish to improve your communication it helps to understand this dynamic relation between word and act. Gifts of oratory or an elegant style are pleasing accessories, but it is action – what you do – which really gets the message across. Make your communication more about the central action; look on your actions more as communications. Eventually our words should become acts, and our acts our truest words.

10. Strive not only to be understood but to understand – be a good listener

Few of us are perfect listeners. Not many of us understand how much we can give to others by the simple act of giving them our whole attention.

One method for improving our powers of understanding is to concentrate on asking questions rather than rushing in with comments. We can also improve our 'feedback': giving others an accurate idea of whether or not we are clear about their meaning, either verbally or by some non-verbal method such as a smile or a nod. Like justice, listening should not only be done: it should be *seen* to be done.

13 Summary

Personal reminders

Effective speaking – six key principles:

1 Be clear

2 Be prepared

3 Be simple

4 Be vivid

5 Be natural

6 Be concise

Practical presentation skills require you to:

- profile the occasion, audience and location

- plan and write the presentation

- use visual aids (if appropriate)

- prepare your talk

- rehearse (with others if necessary)

- deliver on the day

Good communicators are skilled at listening by:

- being willing to listen
- hearing the message
- interpreting the meaning
- evaluating carefully
- responding appropriately.

Effective writing has three elements:

1   Structure

2   Layout

3   Style

and also needs the six key principles of:

1   Clarity

2   Planning

3   Preparation

4   Simplicity

5   Vividness

6   Naturalness

7   Conciseness

Now test yourself

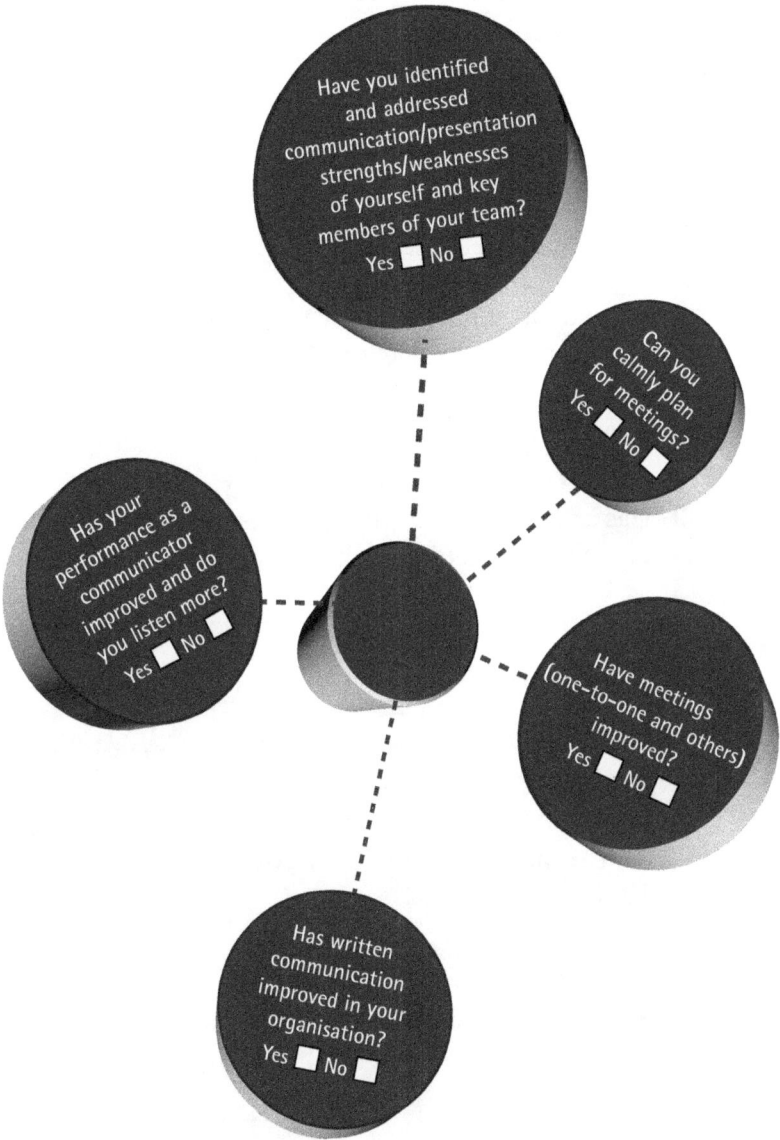

Have you identified
and addressed
communication/presentation
strengths/weaknesses
of yourself and key
members of your team?
Yes ☐ No ☐

Can you
calmly plan
for meetings?
Yes ☐ No ☐

Has your
performance as a
communicator
improved and do
you listen more?
Yes ☐ No ☐

Have meetings
(one-to-one and others)
improved?
Yes ☐ No ☐

Has written
communication
improved in your
organisation?
Yes ☐ No ☐

Checklist: putting the principles of communication to work

Answer yes or no:

1 'You win the match before you run onto the field.' Do you believe this sporting maxim applies to speaking?

_____

2 Do you take time to plan what you are going to say before and during meetings, interviews and telephone calls?

_____

3 Has anyone found anything you have said or written in the last week to be lacking in clarity?

_____

4 Have you taken steps to become a clear thinker?

_____

5 Which of these statements better describe you:

   • 'He/she has a gift for making the complicated sound simple.'

   _____

   • 'He/she tends to turn even the simplest matter into something that is difficult and complicated.'

   _____

- Are you an enthusiastic, interesting and lively speaker? Write 'no' if the following words have been used about you, or anything you have said or written, in the last year:
  - dull
  - boring
  - lifeless
  - lacking creative spark
  - monotonous
  - flat
  - pedestrian

  _____

- Do you find it difficult to relax and be yourself when you are communicating?

  _____

- Have you a reputation for making concise oral contributions and writing succinct letters or memos?

  _____

- Do you find that you are beginning to enjoy the art of communication?

  _____

Appendix 1
Quotes about communication skills

'Speak properly, and in as few words as you can, but always plainly; for the end of speech is not ostentation, but to be understood.'

WILLIAM PENN

'Communication is the art of being

UNDERSTOOD.'

PETER USTINOV

'If any man wishes to write in a clear style, let him first be clear in his thoughts.'

GOETHE

'Have something to say and say it as clearly as you can. That is the only secret of style.'

MATTHEW ARNOLD

'What is conceived well is expressed clearly And words to say it will arise with ease.'

NICHOLAS BOILEAU

'Reading
is to the
mind

what
exercise

is to the
body.'

*'The major mistake in communication
is to believe that it happens'*

GEORGE BERNARD SHAW

On enthusiasm – the life-giver

Enthusiasm consists of a permanent intense delight in what is happening in the life around us at all times, combined with a passionate determination to create something from it, some order, some pattern, some artefacts, with gusto and delight. It means attacking problems, puzzles and obstacles with gumption and with relish.

We can develop this drive in ourselves by consciously looking for the enthralling, the exciting, the enchanting, the emotionally moving in even the most routine or most trivial matters, and apply ourselves to it and with all the vigour of which we are capable. We don't have to display a frenzy of histrionics and so become a menace to our friends. But we do need to enjoy unashamedly and uninhibitedly whatever we are doing.

JOHN CASSON, 'ARE YOU GETTING THROUGH?'
INDUSTRIAL SOCIETY, NOVEMBER 1970

Effortless grace

Many things – such as loving, going to sleep or behaving unaffectedly – are done worst when we try hardest to do them.

C.S. LEWIS, STUDIES IN MEDIEVAL AND RENAISSANCE LITERATURE

The skills of listening

'The fact that people are born with two eyes and two ears, but only one tongue', wrote the Marquise de Sévigné, 'suggests they ought to look and listen twice as much as they speak.'

MARQUISE DE SÉVIGNÉ

Empathy through listening

If a conference... is to result in the exchange of
ideas, we need to pay particular heed to our listening
habits... Living in a competitive culture, most of us are
most of the time chiefly concerned with getting our
own views across, and we tend to find other people's
speeches a tedious interruption of the flow
of our own ideas. Hence, it is necessary to emphasise
that listening does not mean simply maintaining a
polite silence while you are rehearsing in your mind
the speech you are going to make the next time you
can grab a conversational opening. Nor does listening
mean waiting alertly for the flaws in other fellow's
arguments so that later you can mow him down.
Listening means trying to see the problem the way the
speaker sees it – which means not sympathy, which is
feeling for him, but empathy, which is experiencing
with him. Listening requires entering actively and
imaginatively into the other fellow's situation and
trying to understand a frame of reference different
from your own. This is not always an easy task.

S.I. HAYAKAWA

A wise old owl sat in an oak,

The more he heard, the less he spoke;

The less he spoke, the more he heard.

Why aren't we all like that wise old bird?

ANON

'Great listening is within our grasp Give us grace to listen well.'

JOHN KEBLE

Good manners through listening

Essentially style resembles good manners.
It comes of endeavouring to understand others,
of thinking for them rather than yourself – of
thinking, that is, with the heart as well as the
head... So (says Fénelon)... 'your words will be
fewer and more effectual, and while you make
less ado, what you do will be more profitable.'

SIR ARTHUR QUILLER-COUCH
MADE THIS POINT IN THE ART OF WRITING (1916)

Brevity

To do our work we all have to read a mass of papers. Nearly all of them are far too long. This wastes time, while energy has to be spent in looking for essential points.

I ask my colleagues and staff to see that their reports are shorter.

1. The aim should be reports which set out the main points in a series of short, crisp paragraphs.

2. If a report relies on detailed analysis of some complicated factors or on statistics, these should be set out in an appendix.

3. Often the occasion is best met by submitting not a full report, but a reminder consisting of headings only, which can be expounded orally if needed.

4. Let us have an end to such phrases as these: 'it is also important to bear in mind the following considerations... or consideration should be given to the possibility of carrying into effect...' Most of these woolly phrases are mere padding, which can be left out altogether, or replaced by a single word. Let us not shrink from using the short expressive phrase, even if it is conversation.

Reports drawn up on the lines I propose may at first seem rough as compared with the flat surface of officialese jargon, but the saving in time will be great, while the discipline of setting out the real points concisely will prove an aid to clearer thinking.

WINSTON CHURCHILL, 9 AUGUST 1940

'A flame should be lighted
at the commencement and
kept alive with unremitting
splendour to the end.'

MICHAEL FARADAY, ADVICE TO A LECTURER

But of a good leader, who talks little,

When his work is done, his aim fulfilled,

They will all say, 'We did this

ourselves'.

LAO TZU

The effective chairman

The Prime Minister shouldn't speak too much himself in Cabinet. He should start the show or ask somebody else to do so, and then intervene only to bring out the more modest chaps who, despite their seniority, might say nothing if not asked.

And the Prime Minister must sum up... particularly when a non-Cabinet minister is asked to attend, especially if it is his first time, the Prime Minister may have to be cruel. The visitor may want to show how good he is, and go on too long. A good thing is to take no chance and ask him to send the Cabinet a paper in advance... if somebody else looks like making a speech, it is sound to nip in with, 'Are you objecting? You're not? Right. Next business', and the Cabinet can move on leaving in its wake a trail of clear, crisp uncompromising decisions. That is what government is about. And the challenge to democracy is to get it done quickly.

CLEMENT ATTLEE

Examples of good and bad communication

Examples of good communication

Keep it simple

Former British Prime Minister Harold Macmillan once related how after his maiden speech in the Commons, his legendary predecessor David Lloyd George – one of the great political orators of the century – asked him to come and see him. Lloyd George complimented Macmillan on his first attempt and then gave him a tip: 'If you are an ordinary Member of Parliament, make only one point in your speech (you can make it in different ways but it should centre on one point). If you are a minister, you may make two. Only if you are a Prime Minister, can you afford to make three points.'

Encouraging two-way communication

At times I received advice from friends, urging me to give up or curtail visits to troops. They correctly stated that, so far as the mass of men was concerned, I could never speak, personally, to more than a tiny percentage. They argued, therefore, that I was merely wearing myself out, without accomplishing anything significant, so far as the whole Army was concerned. With this I did not agree. In the first place I felt that through constant talking to enlisted men I gained accurate impressions of their state of mind. I talked to them about anything and everything: a favourite question of mine was to inquire whether the particular squad or platoon had figured out any new trick or gadget for use in infantry fighting. I would talk about anything so long as I could get the soldier to talk to me in return.

I knew, of course, that news of a visit with even a few men in a division would soon spread throughout the unit. This, I felt, would encourage men to talk to their superiors, and this habit, I believe, promotes efficiency. There is, among the mass of individuals who carry the rifles in war, a great amount of ingenuity and initiative. If men can naturally and without restraint talk to their officers, the products of their resourcefulness becomes available to all. More-over, out of the habit grows mutual confidence, a feeling of partnership that is the essence of esprit de corps. An army fearful of its officers is never as good as one that trusts and confides in its leaders.

General Dwight D. Eisenhower

Examples of bad communication – the charge of the Light Brigade

To appreciate and learn from this disaster it is necessary for the reader to know the essentials of the situation. The Russians in the Crimean War were attempting to intervene in the siege operations before Sebastopol by cutting the British lines of communication to the seaport of Balaclava. The successful charge of the Heavy Brigade and the stubborn defensive resistance of some infantry regiments checked the Russians, but then Lord Raglan, the Allied Commander, spied the enemy attempting to remove some abandoned guns from some high ground to his right. The country is hilly and divided by valleys. Raglan's command post was on the high ground at the head of the long winding North Valley. The Russians occupied the heights on either side of it, and over a mile away, at its other open end, their cavalry was regrouping behind twelve guns. The Light Brigade stood quite near Raglan but almost on the floor of the valley (see the following map).

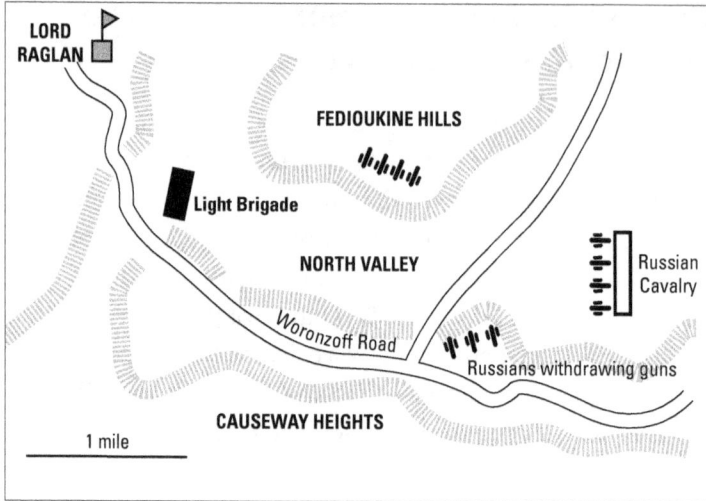

Throughout the story it may be helpful for the reader to bear constantly in mind the simple fact that it was the guns on the Causeway Heights that Raglan wished the Light Brigade to secure – not those guarding the Russian cavalry at the end of North Valley. How did Lucan set out towards the wrong objective – and to tragedy? Cecil Woodham-Smith's account is worth studying closely; it is an unforgettable parable of bad communication:

The charge of the Heavy Brigade ended the second period of the battle. The aspect of the action had been entirely changed by Scarlett's feat. There was no longer any question of the Russians penetrating to Balaclava, they had been pushed away from Balaclava, even out of the South Valley altogether, and at the moment their position presented difficulties. They held the Causeway Heights and the redoubts, and they had infantry and artillery on the Fedioukine Hills on the other side of the North Valley, but between them the North Valley, 1000 yards wide, was empty of troops. The troops holding the captured redoubts on the ridge of the Causeway Heights had therefore little support, and Lord Raglan saw that this was the moment to recover the redoubts, the Causeway Heights, and, with the Heights, the Woronzoff Road.

The two divisions of infantry ordered down two hours earlier should now have come into action, but, though the 1st Division under the Duke of Cambridge was present, the 4th Division under Sir George Cathcart lagged behind. He was still in a bad temper, and as he unwillingly left the Heights, General Airey had brought him orders to assault and recapture the redoubts – So, he thought, his division, straight from the trenches and exhausted, was to attack, while the Guards were merely marched in support along the valley below. He refused to hurry.

Lord Raglan's anger was evident; indeed, William Howard Russell noticed that Lord Raglan had lost his usual marble calm and seemed fidgety and uneasy, continually turning his glasses this way and that and conferring with General Airey and General Estcourt. He now sent Lord Lucan a third order, of which two versions exist. The copy which Lord Raglan retained in his possession runs: 'Cavalry to advance and take advantage of any opportunity to recover the Heights. They will be supported by infantry, which have been ordered to advance on two fronts.' The order as it reached Lord Lucan and was retained by him is slightly different. The final sentence is divided into two. After the word 'ordered' there is a full stop and 'advance' is written with a capital 'A', so that the finals words read 'They will be supported by the infantry which have been ordered. Advance on two fronts.' The change does not affect the issue. Lord Raglan expected Lucan to understand from the order that he was to advance and recapture the redoubts at once without waiting for infantry support, but that infantry had been ordered, and could be expected later.

Lord Lucan read the order in precisely the opposite sense. He was to advance when supported by infantry. Not only did the words of Lord Raglan's order seem to him to have this meaning, by Raglan's treatment of the cavalry throughout the campaign made it highly improbable that he would order an attack by cavalry alone. Again and again, at the Bulganek, at and after the Alma, on October 7th, the cavalry had been restrained, recalled, forbidden to take the offensive, prohibited from engaging the enemy. Only an hour or so ago Lord Raglan had withdrawn the cavalry from their position at the entrance to Balaclava, where they were preparing to engage the Russian cavalry, and placed them in an inactive position under the Heights. It never crossed Lucan's mind that he was expected to launch an attack by cavalry with the prospect of being supported at some future time by the infantry. He mounted his division, moved the Light Brigade over to a position across the end of the North Valley, drew up the Heavy Brigade on the Woronzoff Road, behind them and on the right, and waited for the infantry, which in his own words 'had not yet arrived'.

Ten minutes, a quarter of an hour, half an hour passed, and the infantry did not appear. Three-quarters of an hour passed, and still Lord Lucan waited. The attack which Lord Raglan wished the cavalry to make appeared to border on recklessness. Redoubt No. 1, on the crown of Canroberts Hills, was inaccessible to horsemen. Nos. 2 and 3 would have to be charged uphill in the face of infantry and artillery. The Heavy Brigade had earlier come within range of the guns in No. 2 and had been forced to retire. However, Lord Raglan, with his power to divine the temper of troops, perceived that the whole Russian Army had been shaken by the triumphant and audacious charge of the Heavy Brigade and that, threatened again by British cavalry, they would retire. Conversations with Russian officers after the war proved Lord Raglan to be right. A feeling of depression had spread through the Russian Army as they saw their great and, as they believed, unconquerable mass of horse-men break and fly before a handful of the Heavy Brigade. For the moment the British possessed a moral ascendancy, but the moment must be swiftly turned to account, and up on the Heights there were murmurs of impatience and indignation as no further action followed the triumph of the Heavy Brigade, and down below Lord Lucan and the cavalry continued to sit motionless in the saddles.

Suddenly along the lines of the Causeway Ridge there was activity. Through glasses teams of artillery horses with lasso tackle could be made out; they were coming up to the redoubts, and a buzz of excitement broke out among the staff. 'By Jove! They're going to take away the guns' – the British naval guns with which the redoubts had been armed.

Captured guns were the proof of victory: Lord Raglan would find it difficult to explain away Russian claims to have inflicted a defeat on him if the Russians had not only taken an important position, but captured guns as well. The removal of the guns must be prevented, and, calling General Airey, Lord Raglan gave him rapid instructions. General Airey scribbled an order in pencil on a piece of paper resting on his sabretache and read it to Lord Raglan, who dictated some additional words.

This was the 'fourth order' issued to Lord Lucan on the day of Balaclava – the order which resulted in the Charge of the Light Brigade – and the original still exists. The paper is of poor quality, the lines are hurriedly written in pencil and the flimsy sheet has a curiously insignificant and shabby appearance. The wording of the order runs: 'Lord Raglan wishes the cavalry to advance rapidly to the front – follow the enemy and try to prevent the enemy carrying away the guns. Troop Horse Artillery may accompany. French cavalry is on your left. Immediate (Sgd.) Airey.'

Captain Thomas Leslie, a member of the family of Leslie of Glaslough, was the next aide-de-camp for duty, and the order had been placed in his hand when Nolan Intervened. The honour of carrying the order he claimed was his, by virtue of his superior rank and consummate horsemanship. The only road now available from the Heights to the plain 600 or 700 feet below was little more than a track down the face of a precipice, and speed was of vital importance. Lord Raglan gave way and Nolan, snatching the paper out of Captain Leslie's hand, galloped off. Just as Nolan was about to descend, Lord Raglan called out to him, 'Tell Lord Lucan the cavalry is to attack immediately.' Nolan plunged over the verge of the Heights at breakneck speed.

Any other horseman would have picked his way with care down that rough, precipitous slope, but Nolan spurred his horse, and up on the Heights the watchers held their breathe as, slithering, scrambling, stumbling, he rushed down to the plain.

So far the day had been a terrible one for Edward Nolan; even its sole glory, the charge of the Heavy Brigade, had been gall and wormwood to his soul. He was a light-cavalryman, believing passionately in the superior efficiency of light over heavy horsemen – 'so unwieldy, so encumbered', he had written – and in this, the first cavalry action of the campaign, the light cavalry had done absolutely nothing. Hour after hour, in an agony of impatience, he had watched the Light Cavalry Brigade standing by, motionless, inglorious and, as onlookers had not scrupled to say, shamefully inactive.

For this he furiously blamed Lord Lucan, as he had furiously blamed Lord Lucan on every other occasion when the cavalry had been kept out of action, 'raging', in William Howard Russell's phrase, against him all over the camp. Irish-Italian, excitable, headstrong, recklessly courageous, Nolan was beside himself with irritation and anger as he swooped like an avenging angel from the Heights, bearing the order which would force the man he detested and despised to attack at last.

With a sign of relief the watchers saw him arrive safely, gallop furiously across the plain and, with his horse trembling, sweating and blown from the wild descent, hand the order to Lord Lucan sitting in the saddle between his two brigades. Lucan opened and read it.

The order appeared to him to be utterly obscure. Lord Raglan and General Airey had forgotten that they were looking down from 600 feet. Not only could they survey the whole action, but the inequalities of the plain disappeared when viewed from above. Lucan from his position could see nothing; inequalities of the ground concealed the activity round the redoubts, no single enemy soldier was in sight; nor had he any picture of the movements of the enemy in his mind's eye, because he had unaccountably neglected to take any steps to acquaint himself with the Russian dispositions. He should, after receiving the third order, have made it his business to make some form of reconnaissance; he should when he found he could see nothing from his position, have shifted his ground – but he did not.

He read the order 'carefully', with the fussy deliberateness which maddened his staff, while Nolan quivered with impatience at his side. It seemed to Lord Lucan that the order was not only obscure but absurd: artillery was to be attacked by cavalry; infantry support was not mentioned; it was elementary that cavalry charging artillery in such circumstances must be annihilated. In his own account of these fatal moments Lucan says that he 'hesitated and urged the uselessness of such an attack and the dangers attending it'; but Nolan, almost insane with impatience, cut him short and 'in a most authoritative tone' repeated the final message he had been given on the Height: 'Lord Raglan's orders are that the cavalry are to attack immediately.'

For such a tone to be used by an aide-de-camp to a Lieutenant-General was unheard of; moreover, Lord Lucan was perfectly aware that Nolan detested him and habitually abused him. It would have been asking a very great deal of any man to keep his temper in such circumstances, and Lord Lucan's temper was violent. He could see nothing, 'neither enemy nor guns being in sight', he wrote, nor did he in the least understand what the order meant. It was said later that Lord Raglan intended the third and fourth orders to be read together, and that the instruction in the third order to advance and recover the Heights made it clear that the guns mentioned in the fourth order must be on those Heights. Lord Lucan, however, read the two orders separately. He turned angrily on Nolan, 'Attack, sir? Attack what? What guns, sir?'

The crucial moment had arrived. Nolan threw back his head, and, 'in a most disrespectful and significant manner', flung out his arm and, with a furious gesture, pointed, not to the Causeway Heights and the redoubts with the captured British guns, but to the end of the North Valley, where the Russian cavalry routed by the Heavy Brigade were now established with their guns in front of them. 'There, my lord, is you enemy; there are your guns,' he said, and with those words and that gesture the doom of the Light Brigade was sealed.

What did Nolan mean? It has been maintained that his gesture was merely a taunt, that he had no intention of indicating any direction, and that Lord Lucan, carried away by rage, read a meaning into an out-flung arm which was never there.

The truth will never be known, because a few minutes later Nolan was killed, but his behaviour in that short interval indicates that he did believe the attack was to be down the North Valley and on those guns with which the Russian cavalry routed by the Heavy Brigade had been allowed to retire.

It is not difficult to account for such a mistake. Nolan, the cavalry enthusiast and a cavalry commander of talent, was well aware that a magnificent opportunity had been lost when the Light Brigade failed to pursue after the charge of the Heavies. It was, indeed, the outstanding, the flagrant error of the day, and he must have watched with fury and despair as the routed Russians were suffered to withdraw in safety with the much-desired trophies, their guns. When he received the fourth order he was almost off his head with excitement and impatience, and he misread it. He leapt to the joyful conclusion that at last vengeance was to be taken on those Russians who had been suffered to escape. He had not carried the third order, and read by itself the wording of the fourth was ambiguous. Moreover, Lord Raglan's last words to him, 'Tell Lord Lucan that the cavalry is to attack immediately', were fatally lacking in precision.

And so he plunged down the Heights and with a contemptuous gesture, scorning the man who in his opinion was responsible for the wretched mishandling of the cavalry, he pointed down the North Valley. 'There, my lord, is your enemy; there are your guns.'

Lord Lucan felt himself to be in a hideous dilemma. His resentment against Lord Raglan was indescribable; the orders he had received during the battle had been, in his opinion, not only idiotic and ambiguous, but insulting. He had been treated, he wrote later, like a subaltern. He had been peremptorily ordered out of his first position – the excellent position chosen in conjunction with Sir Colin Campbell – consequently after the charge of the Heavies there had been no pursuit. He had received without explanation a vague order to wait for infantry. What infantry? Now came this latest order to take his division and charge to certain death. Throughout the campaign he had had bitter experience of orders from Lord Raglan, and now he foresaw ruin; but he was helpless. The Queen's Regulations laid down that 'all orders sent by aides-de-camp... are to be obeyed with the same readiness, as if delivered personally by the general officers to whom such aides are attached'. The Duke of Wellington himself had laid this down. Had Lord Lucan refused to execute an order brought by a member of the Headquarters staff and delivered with every assumption of authority he would, in his own words, have had no choice but 'to blow his brains out'.

Nolan's manner had been so obviously insolent that observers thought he would be placed under arrest. Lord Lucan, however, merely shrugged his shoulders and, turning his back on Nolan, trotted off alone, to where Lord Cardigan was sitting in front of the Light Brigade.

Nolan then rode over to his friend Captain Morris, who was sitting in his saddle in front of the 17th Lancers – the same Captain Morris who had urged Lord Cardigan to pursue earlier in the day – and received permission to ride beside him in the charge.

There was now a pause of several minutes, and it is almost impossible to believe that Nolan, sitting beside his close friend and sympathizer, did not disclose the objective of the charge. If Nolan had believed the attack was to be on the Causeway Heights and the redoubts, he must surely have told Captain Morris. Morris, however, who survived the charge though desperately wounded, believed the attack was to be on the guns at the end of the North Valley.

Meanwhile Lord Lucan, almost for the first time, was speaking directly and personally to Lord Cardigan. Had the two men not detested each other so bitterly, had they been able to examine the order together and discuss its meaning, the Light Brigade might have been saved. Alas, thirty years of hatred could not be bridged; each, however, observed perfect military courtesy. Holding the order in his hand, Lord Lucan informed Lord Cardigan of the contents and ordered him to advance down the North Valley with the Light Brigade, while he himself followed in support with the heavy Brigade.

Lord Cardigan now took an astonishing step. Much as he hated the man before him, rigid as were his ideas of military etiquette, he remonstrated with his superior officer. Bringing down his sword in salute he said, 'Certainly, sir; but allow me to point out to you that the Russians have a battery in the valley on our front, and batteries and riflemen on both sides.'

Lord Lucan once more shrugged his shoulders. 'I know it,' he said; 'but Lord Raglan will have it. We have no choice but to obey.' Lord Cardigan made no further comment, but saluted again. Lord Lucan then instructed him to 'advance very steadily and keep his men well in hand'. Lord Cardigan saluted once more, wheeled his horse and rode over to his second-in-command, Lord George Paget, remarking aloud to himself as he did so, 'Well, here goes the last of the Brudenells.'

How not to deal with redundancies

'Good morning, welcome to this full English breakfast. From the rumours you may have heard you will all know why you are here. For two months a team from our head office in Dayton, Ohio, have been assessing us. You will have seen them in the corridors and accessing your computers. Two breakfasts have been arranged, one tomorrow for those who are staying and this… Please do not return to your offices, the security staff are clearing out your personal possessions. The Managing Director has just telephoned in to say that he has overslept, so I will hand you straight over to our solicitor who will outline the legal minimum of redundancy terms we are forced to give you…'

'This should be called the Last Supper,' said Sally grimly to her neighbour as she pushed away her plate. 'Somehow I don't feel like bacon and eggs this morning. Pass the black coffee.'

Appendix 3
Tricks of the trade

Professional performers

- Work with their nerves because adrenaline can be harnessed to boost your performance

- Focus on breathing (to stop nerves overbalancing and to keep them under control)

- Use voice warm-ups

- Use individuals at random in an audience to speak to

- Keep hands still unless they can be used with confidence

- Vary their speaking tone and volume

- Speak with feeling

- Imagine they are communicating with the person in a simple conversational style

- Concentrate on what is being said

- Practice out loud

- Are familiar with their own voice

- Know the duration of their performance

- Hone their speeches as well as practice and rehearse to perfection, memorising key words/phrases

- Pause appropriately and never gabble

Hints from professional communicators

1 Sultan Kermally: Management consultant, writer and lecturer

1 COMMUNICATION SKILLS

- Select words carefully

- Establish effective channels of communication

- Make each manager responsible for effective communication their area

- Ask for feedback

- Listen very carefully

- Interpret and evaluate feedback

- Empathise with your staff

- Reflect enthusiasm in relation to the subject matter of communication

2 MAKING PRESENTATIONS

- Prepare. Be familiar with your material
- Rehearse. This is important
- Walk confidently to the lectern. Do not use it as your psychological crutch
- Arrange your notes
- Establish eye contact with your audience
- Resist the temptation to speak fast
- Pace your voice. Change your pitch and volume
- Speak clearly

3 NEGOTIATING SUCCESSFULLY

- Establish 'rapport' with the other party. Reflect your positive attitude and at the outset state that you are after a win-win situation. Be prepared with some conversation openers.

- Ask open questions to explore statements being made. Listen very carefully to what is being said and observe body language and the tone of the communication.

- When making your offer explain your reasons behind it and indicate that it is not a 'take it or leave it' offer. If the other party makes an offer ask for an explanation and ask closed questions to make sure you understand the offer being made.

- Propose trade-offs and make concessions gracefully without implying and weakness. Come to some resolution but if you do have to disagree, do so without being disagreeable.

- If you arrive at deadlocks, focus on the problem. Limit the problem and take a break to rethink the situation.

- Focus on the area of agreement and come to mutually satisfactory conclusions in certain aspects of your negotiation.

2 Gerry Kushel: Presentation skills expert, speaker and psychotherapist

1 MANAGE YOURSELF THROUGH EFFECTIVE THINKING

- You'd worry a whole lot less about the other people (the audience) are thinking of you if only you knew how rarely they did.

- Don't sweat over the small stuff. (The speech that you are giving.) It's all small stuff.

- People (the audience) will treat you the way you teach them to treat you.

- I want to give an excellent speech, not a perfect one.

- This too shall pass.

- The best is yet to come.

- These people love me.

- I'm bearing gifts to bring to these people.

- I prefer to give a great talk, I don't need to.

- This talk is a project, not a problem.

- Be realistic about the objectives and success of this talk, not merely reasonable.

- It's not the real me that is being judged during this talk, just my image.

- Public speaking is just a game, play the game to win.

- I did this before, so I can do it again.

- Modulate your voice. A deeper resonant tone generally commands more respect.

- Use self-confident body language. Create a command presence.

- Dress for success.

- Create a warm tone.

2 MANAGE YOUR MATERIAL

- Break down your material so that your audience will appreciate your message.

- Keep things uncomplicated.

- Adopt the rule of K-I-S-S. 'Keep it simple, stupid.'

3 MANAGING YOUR AUDIENCE

- Have friendly eye contact with various parts of the audience, not just to one side or another.

- Mingle a bit with some members of the audience in advance for them to warm to you.

- Move a bit when you are speaking, but not as a distraction. Don't be an automatic prisoner of the podium.

- Assume that you are bearing gifts for the audience. Find a friendly face or two and be responsive.

- Feel as if the members of the audience are guests in your home. Make them comfortable.

- Speak loudly enough so that those in the back row can definitely hear you.

- Don't talk too long. Break up your talk, if possible, with syndicate/buzz sessions, questions and answers, dyads and triads.

Other John Adair titles by Thorogood

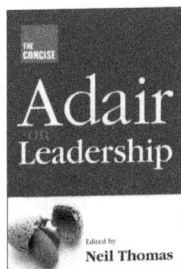

The Concise Adair on Leadership

Edited by Neil Thomas

Paperback ISBN: 978 185418 9219
Ebook ISBN: 978 185418 9226

This book is a master-class on the art of leadership. While management fads come and go John Adair's work remains a beacon of practical advice and shrewd insight. This book encapsulates his writing on how to develop your own leadership potential, to motivate your colleagues and to build a creative and high-performance team.

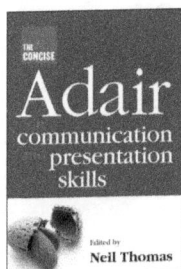

The Concise Adair on Creativity and Innovation

Edited by Neil Thomas

Paperback ISBN: 978 185418 9257
Ebook ISBN: 978 185418 9264

This book is a goldmine of practical advice and shrewd insight. John Adair summarises everything you need to know in order to understand creative processes, eliminate obstacles and build on good ideas. He provides techniques to build confidence in your own creative skills and also gives practical advice on how to tolerate uncertainty and participate creatively as a team member or leader. In short, learn how to innovate and put great ideas into action.

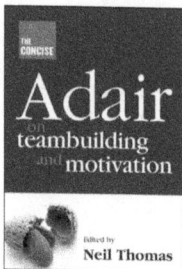

The Concise Adair on Teambuilding and Motivation

Edited by Neil Thomas

Paperback ISBN: 978 185418 9271
Ebook ISBN: 978 185418 9288

This book encapsulates John Adair's writing on teambuilding and motivational skills in one easy to refer to master-class. These skills are of crucial importance in business and the leadership role in particular. Managers and leaders must be effective team builders and motivators to be able to achieve their business aims and get the best out of people. This book develops Adair's classic theory on Team, Task and Individual, and summarises all his writing on leaders and motivation and getting the best from people. It includes sections on being self-motivated, selecting people, target setting and reward and recognition.

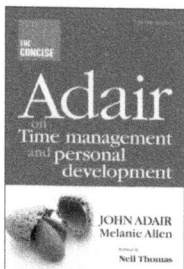

The Concise Adair on Time Management and Personal Development

John Adair and Melanie Allen

Paperback ISBN: 978 185418 9295
Ebook ISBN: 978 185418 9301

John Adair's wide experience of management development adds a depth of insight and context to the practical advice in this book. It covers practical advice and skills on how to establish clear long-term goals and link your daily action planning to their achievement. It provides the tools, techniques and framework for continuing personal development so you can build a truly successful career.

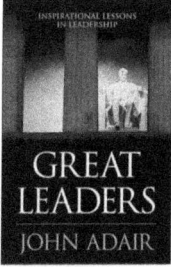

Great Leaders – Inspirational Lessons in Leadership

John Adair

Paperback ISBN: 978 185418 9172
Ebook ISBN: 978 185418 9189

John Adair asks, who are the great leaders in history and what have they got to teach us today about the nature and practice of leadership? In asking to what degree true leadership can be identified and developed, he explores the make-up and achievements of leaders as diverse as Lao Tzu and Machiavelli, Margaret Thatcher and Mandela.

Using a thematic structure, John Adair illustrates different facets of leadership, and examines the very different styles of leadership; he explores the cardinal qualities of inspiring, communicating and decision making but he also touches on the value of humour, intuition and imagination.

This is a thought-provoking book, rich in example and wide-ranging in scope: key qualities that so often appear abstract ideals – motivation, communication, decision-making, inspiration – here almost literally come to life.

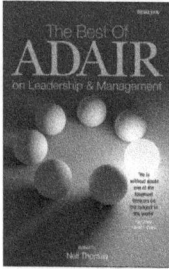

The Best of John Adair on Leadership and Management

Edited by Neil Thomas

Paperback ISBN: 978 185418 9196
Ebook ISBN: 978 185418 9202

Here in one book is a brilliant summary of all John Adair's ideas, advice and techniques. The book is a clearly written master-class on:

· Growing into an effective and inspiring leader

· How to build a cohesive and responsive team

· Techniques of creativity and innovation

· Effective analysis and decision-making

· Mastering the art of good communication

· Managing your own time, managing yourself

The book is packed with practical guidance and insights, helpful charts, diagrams and forms.

To see a full listing of all Thorogood books go to:
www.thorogoodpublishing.co.uk

All titles can be ordered via the Thorogood website or direct from Amazon.

As well as publishing books which are accessible, practical and of immediate value, we also provide business and legal training events to support your skills development and learning needs.

Falconbury

Falconbury specialise in skills development for individuals and teams across all types of organisations, large and small, public and private, domestic and international. We run a large portfolio of events in a variety of formats from five-day industry-specific 'MBA-style' programmes to one, two or three-day courses – all of which can be delivered face to face or via a webinar platform.

All our public courses can also be run as tailored programmes for organisations anywhere in the world via a webinar platform or at a location of your choice. The programmes can be 'off the shelf', or we can work with you to create a bespoke training solution to meet your exact needs.

Finally, we also offer individual coaching and event management solutions.

With over 800 internationally renowned presenters, trainers, consultants, industry leaders and authors as training partners, Falconbury can deliver an all-encompassing international training and consultancy service.

To see our full portfolio of events go to **www.falconbury.co.uk** or, to discuss your particular training needs, please call our team of training advisers on **+44 (0)20 7729 6677**. We look forward to working with you.

Management Forum

For over 30 years Management Forum has been an internationally renowned independent training company that organises professional conferences, seminars and in-house courses for the pharmaceutical, life science and intellectual property sectors. Our aim is to provide you with the highest quality events that update you with the very latest information and are relevant and important to both you and your company.

We pride ourselves on our links to the best and most knowledgeable expert speakers in your business sector. We believe in bringing you together with your peers in order to learn, engage, share and network with the very best, whether that's face to face or via a webinar platform.

We are experts in knowing the experts you will want to hear from and have been bringing you this expertise since 1983. To see our full portfolio of events go to: **www.management-forum.co.uk** or, to discuss your particular training needs, please call our team of training advisers on **+44 (0)20 7749 4730**. We look forward to hearing from you.